·Cooking for Today·

PASTA DISHES

·Cooking for Today·

PASTA DISHES

PAMELA WESTLAND

SIENA

A Siena Book
Siena is an imprint of Parragon Books

First published in Great Britain in 1996 by
Parragon Book Service Ltd
Unit 13-17, Avonbridge Trading Estate
Atlantic Road
Avonmouth
Bristol BS11 9QD

ISBN 0-7525-1494-6

Printed in Italy

Acknowledgements:

Design & DTP: Pedro & Frances Prá-Lopez / Kingfisher Design
Art Direction: Lisa Tai
Managing Editor: Alexa Stace
Special Photography: Amanda Heywood
Home Economist: Carol Hanslip
Stylist: Marian Price

Gas Hob supplied by New World Domestic Appliances Ltd
Photographs on pages 6, 20, 40 & 60: By courtesy of ZEFA

Note:
Cup measurements in this book are for American cups. Tablespoons are assumed to be 15ml.

Contents

First Courses

Pasta dishes perfectly fulfil the requirements of an opening course – to give family and friends an immediate feeling of well-being; to delight the eye, and excite but not dull the palate.

This is the time to serve clear but hearty soups contrasting the colours, textures and flavours of crisp, fresh vegetables and short pasta shapes; for a burst of mingled flavours such as those of roasted vegetables or spicy sausage, and for subtle, creamy sauces with herbs and nuts.

Serve the first course in the prettiest dishes you have, in scallop shells, or on glass plates. Serve hot dishes piping hot, cold ones refreshingly, tinglingly cold. Garnish each one with a leaf or a sprig or two of herbs, and serve them with a choice of breads in the Mediterranean style: long, crisp grissini breadsticks, olive ciabatta bread or warm baguettes.

Opposite: *An Italian fisherman and his wife inspect the nets. A wide variety of fish and shellfish are caught in the seas around the Italian coast, and this abundance is reflected in the antipasto dishes, which often include fish soups and seafood salads.*

STEP 1

STEP 2

STEP 3

STEP 4

HARICOT BEAN & PASTA SOUP

A dish with proud Mediterranean origins, this soup is a winter warmer, to be served with warm, crusty bread and, if you like, a slice of cheese.

SERVES 4

250 g/8 oz/generous 1 cup dried haricot
  beans, soaked, drained and rinsed (see
  below)
4 tbsp olive oil
2 large onions, sliced
3 garlic cloves, chopped
1 x 425 g/15 oz can chopped tomatoes
1 tsp dried oregano
1 tsp tomato purée (paste)
900 ml/1¹⁄₂ pints/3¹⁄₂ cups water
90 g/3 oz small pasta shapes, such as fusilli
  or conchigliette
125 g/4 oz sun-dried tomatoes, drained and
  thinly sliced
1 tbsp chopped coriander, or flat-leaved
  parsley
2 tbsp grated Parmesan
salt and pepper

1 Put the soaked beans into a large pan, cover with cold water and bring them to the boil. Boil rapidly for 15 minutes, to remove any harmful toxins. Drain the beans in a colander.

2 Heat the oil in a pan over a medium heat and fry the onions until they are just beginning to change colour. Stir in the garlic and cook for 1 further minute. Stir in the chopped tomatoes, oregano and the tomato purée and and pour on the water. Add the beans, bring to the boil and cover the pan. Simmer for 45 minutes, or until the beans are almost tender.

3 Add the pasta, season the soup and stir in the sun-dried tomatoes. Return the soup to the boil, partly cover the pan and continue cooking for 10 minutes, or until the pasta is nearly tender.

4 Stir in the chopped herb. Taste the soup and adjust the seasoning if necessary. Transfer to a warmed soup tureen to serve, sprinkled with the cheese. Serve hot.

DRIED BEANS

You can soak the dried beans for several hours or overnight in a large bowl of cold water. Or, if it is more convenient, place them in a pan of cold water and bring them to the boil. Remove the pan from the heat and leave the beans to cool in the water. Drain and rinse the beans before beginning the recipe.

STEP 2

STEP 3

STEP 4

STEP 5

CHICKEN SCALLOPS

Served in scallop shells, this makes a stylish presentation for a dinner-party first course.

SERVES 4

175 g/6 oz short-cut macaroni, or other
    short pasta shapes
3 tbsp vegetable oil, plus extra for brushing
1 medium onion, finely chopped
3 rashers unsmoked collar or back bacon,
    rind removed, chopped
125 g/4 oz button mushrooms, thinly sliced
    or chopped
175 g/6 oz/³/₄ cup cooked chicken, diced
175 ml/6 fl oz/³/₄ cup crème fraîche
4 tbsp dry breadcrumbs
60 g/2 oz/¹/₂ cup Cheddar cheese, grated
salt and pepper
flat-leaved parsley sprigs, to garnish

1 Cook the pasta in a large pan of boiling salted water to which you have added 1 tablespoon of the oil. When the pasta is almost tender, drain in a colander, return to the pan and cover.

2 Heat the grill to medium. Heat the remaining oil in a pan over medium heat and fry the onion until it is translucent. Add the chopped bacon and mushrooms and cook for a further 3-4 minutes, stirring once or twice.

3 Stir in the pasta, chicken and crème fraîche and season.

4 Brush 4 large scallop shells with oil. Spoon in the chicken mixture and smooth to make neat mounds.

5 Mix together the breadcrumbs and cheese and sprinkle over the top of the shells. Press the topping lightly into the chicken mixture, and grill for 4-5 minutes, until golden brown and bubbling. Garnish with parsley, and serve hot.

ALTERNATIVE

If you do not have scallop shells, you can assemble this dish in four small ovenproof dishes, such as ramekin dishes, or in one large one.

STEP 1

STEP 2

STEP 3

STEP 4

SPICY SAUSAGE SALAD

A warm sausage and pasta dressing spooned over chilled salad leaves makes a refreshing combination to start a meal.

SERVES 4

125g/4 oz small pasta shapes, such as elbow tubetti
3 tbsp olive oil
1 medium onion, chopped
1 small yellow (bell) pepper, cored, seeded and cut into matchstick strips
175 g/6 oz spicy pork sausage such as chorizo, skinned and sliced
2 tbsp red wine
1 tbsp red wine vinegar
mixed salad leaves, chilled
salt

1 Cook the pasta in a large pan of boiling salted water, adding 1 tablespoon of the oil. When the pasta is almost tender, drain it in a colander and set aside.

2 Heat the remaining oil in a saucepan over a medium heat. Fry the onion until it is translucent, then stir in the garlic, (bell) pepper and sliced sausage and cook for 3-4 minutes, stirring once or twice.

3 Add the wine, wine vinegar and reserved pasta to the pan, stir to blend well and bring the mixture just to the boil.

4 Arrange the chilled salad leaves on 4 individual serving plates and spoon on the warm sausage and pasta mixture. Serve at once.

SPICED SAUSAGES

Chorizo is a Spanish spiced sausage. Another Spanish sausage to try is merguez, usually very hot. Other sausages to use are the Italian pepperoni, flavoured with chilli peppers, fennel and spices, and one of the many varieties of salami, usually flavoured with garlic and pepper.

STEP 1

STEP 2a

STEP 2b

STEP 3

SPAGHETTI WITH RICOTTA CHEESE

This makes a quick and easy starter, ideal for the summer.

SERVES 4

350 g/12 oz spaghetti
3 tbsp olive oil
45 g/1½ oz/3 tbsp butter, cut into small
  pieces
2 tbsp chopped parsley

SAUCE:
125 g/4 oz/1 cup freshly ground almonds
125 g/4 oz/½ cup Ricotta
large pinch of grated nutmeg
large pinch of ground cinnamon
150 ml/¼ pint/⅔ cup crème fraîche
120 ml/4 fl oz/½ cup hot chicken stock
freshly ground black pepper
1 tbsp pine kernels
coriander leaves, to garnish

1 Cook the spaghetti in a large pan of boiling salted water to which you have added 1 tablespoon of the oil. When it is almost tender, drain the pasta in a colander. Return to the pan and toss with the butter and parsley. Cover the pan and keep warm.

2 To make the sauce, mix together the ground almonds, Ricotta, nutmeg, cinnamon and crème fraîche to make a thick paste. Gradually pour on the remaining oil, stirring constantly

until it is well blended.
Gradually pour on the hot stock, stirring all the time, until the sauce is smooth.

3 Transfer the spaghetti to a warmed serving dish, pour on the sauce and toss well. Sprinkle each serving with pine kernels and garnish with coriander leaves. Serve warm.

TOSSING SPAGHETTI

To toss spaghetti and coat it thoroughly with a sauce or dressing, use the 2 largest forks you can find – special forks aare sold in some kitchen shops just for this purpose. Holding one fork in each hand, ease the prongs under the spaghetti from each side and lift them towards the centre. Repeat evenly and rhythmically until the pasta is well and truly tossed.

STEP 2a

STEP 2b

STEP 2c

STEP 3

CHILLED NOODLES & PEPPERS

This is a convenient dish to serve when you are arriving home just before family or friends. You can have it all prepared and ready to assemble in minutes.

SERVES 4-6

250 g/8 oz ribbon noodles, or Chinese egg noodles
1 tbsp sesame oil
1 red (bell)pepper
1 yellow (bell) pepper
1 green (bell) pepper
6 spring onions (scallions), cut into matchstick strips
salt

DRESSING:
5 tbsp sesame oil
2 tbsp light soy sauce
1 tbsp tahini (sesame paste)
4-5 drops hot pepper sauce

1 Preheat the grill (broiler) to medium. Cook the noodles in a large pan of boiling, salted water until they are almost tender. Drain them in a colander, run cold water through them and drain thoroughly. Tip the noodles into a bowl, stir in the sesame oil, cover and chill.

2 Cook the (bell) peppers under the grill (broiler), turning them frequently, until they are blackened on all sides. Plunge into cold water, then skin them. Cut in half, remove the core and seeds and cut the flesh into thick strips. Set aside in a covered container. To make the dressing, mix together the sesame oil, soy sauce, tahini and hot pepper sauce.

3 Pour the dressing on the noodles, reserving 1 tablespoon, and toss well. Turn the noodles into a serving dish, arrange the grilled (bell) peppers over the noodles and spoon on the reserved dressing. Scatter on the spring onion (scallion) strips.

ALTERNATIVE

If you have time, another way of skinning peppers is to first grill (broil) them, then place in a plastic bag, seal and leave for about 20 minutes. The skin will then peel off easily.

VEGETABLE & PASTA SALAD

*Roasted vegetables and pasta make a delicious, colourful salad,
ideal as a starter or to serve with a platter of cold meats.*

STEP 1

SERVES 4
OVEN: 220°C/450°F/GAS 7

2 small aubergines (eggplant), thinly sliced
1 large onion, sliced
2 large beef-steak tomatoes, skinned and
*   cut into wedges*
1 red (bell) pepper, cored, seeded and sliced
1 fennel bulb, thinly sliced
2 garlic cloves, sliced
4 tbsp olive oil
175 g/6 oz small pasta shapes, such as
*   stars*
90 g/3 oz/$^{1}/_{2}$ cup feta cheese, crumbled
a few basil leaves, torn
salt and pepper
salad leaves, to serve

DRESSING:
5 tbsp olive oil
juice of 1 orange
1 tsp grated orange zest
$^{1}/_{4}$ tsp paprika
4 canned anchovies, finely chopped

1 Place the sliced aubergines (eggplant) in a colander, sprinkle with salt and set them aside for about 1 hour to draw out some of the bitter juices. Rinse under cold, running water to remove the salt, then drain. Toss on paper towels to dry.

2 Arrange the aubergines (eggplant), onion, tomatoes, red (bell) pepper, fennel and garlic in a single layer in an ovenproof dish, sprinkle on 3 tablespoons of the olive oil and season with salt and pepper. Bake in the preheated oven, uncovered, for 45 minutes, until the vegetables begin to turn brown. Remove from the oven and set aside to cool.

3 Cook the pasta in a large pan of boiling salted water to which you have added the remaining olive oil. When the pasta is almost tender, drain it in a colander, then transfer to a bowl.

4 To make the dressing, mix together the olive oil, orange juice, orange zest and paprika. Stir in the finely chopped anchovies and season with pepper. Pour the dressing over the pasta while it is still hot, and toss well. Set the pasta aside to cool.

5 To assemble the salad, line a shallow serving dish with the salad leaves and arrange the cold roasted vegetables in the centre. Spoon the pasta in a ring around the vegetables and scatter over the feta cheese and basil leaves. Serve at once.

STEP 2

STEP 3

STEP 4

19

CHAPTER TWO

Pasta with Meat Sauces

Some of the most popular and widely-known pasta dishes are ones
that bring together long strands of pasta cooked al dente,
and a rich, hearty sauce including beef or lamb,
chicken or ham. Spaghetti Bolognese needs no introduction,
and yet it is said that there are almost as many versions of this
delicious regional dish as there are lovers of Italian food. Our
version includes both beef and bacon in a sauce enriched
with beef stock and red wine.

Layered pasta dishes that are served in slices, wedges or squares are
perfect standbys for parties and picnics, buffet meals or informal
family occasions; children and teenagers love them.
Our selection includes creamy lasagne and Greek pasticcio,
aubergine and pasta cake and an unusual meat loaf
with a contrasting pasta layer; they will all make
worthy additions to your repertoire
of baked pasta favourites.

Opposite: *Verdant landscape
near Bologna, home of some
splendid hams, as well as one of
the best-known pasta sauces –
Bolognese.*

SPAGHETTI CARBONARA

Have all the cooked ingredients as hot as possible, so that the beaten
eggs are cooked on contact. It is a classic dish,
and one to serve with a flourish.

STEP 1

SERVES 4

400 g/14 oz spaghetti
2 tbsp olive oil
1 large onion, thinly sliced
2 garlic cloves, chopped
175 g/6 oz streaky bacon rashers, rind
*   removed, cut into thin strips*
30 g/1 oz/2 tbsp butter
175 g/6 oz mushrooms, thinly sliced
300 ml/¹⁄₂ pint/1¹⁄₄ cups double (heavy)
*   cream*
3 eggs, beaten
90 g/3 oz/³⁄₄ cup grated Parmesan, plus
*   extra to serve, optional*
freshly ground black pepper
sprigs of sage, to garnish

1 Heat a large serving dish or bowl.
Cook the spaghetti in a large pan of
boiling salted water, adding 1 tablespoon
of the oil. When the pasta is almost
tender, drain in a colander. Return the
spaghetti to the pan, cover and leave it in
a warm place.

2 While the spaghetti is cooking,
heat the remaining oil in a frying
pan over a medium heat. Fry the onion
until it is translucent, then add the garlic
and bacon and fry until the bacon
is crisp.

3 Remove the onion, garlic and
bacon with a slotted spoon and set
it aside to keep warm. Heat the butter in
the pan and fry the mushrooms for 3-4
minutes, stirring them once or twice.
Return the bacon mixture to the
mushrooms. Cover and keep warm.

4 Stir together the cream, the beaten
eggs and cheese and season with
salt and pepper.

5 Working very quickly to avoid
cooling the cooked ingredients, tip
the spaghetti into the bacon and
mushroom mixture and pour on the
eggs. Toss the spaghetti quickly, using 2
forks and serve it at once. You can, if you
wish, hand round more grated Parmesan
cheese.

STEP 3

STEP 4

ACCOMPANIMENTS

A chilled salad of mixed leaves such as
young spinach, radicchio and endive
tossed in a vinaigrette dressing makes a
good accompaniment. You may also like
to serve a bowl of chilled radishes.

STEP 5

STEP 1

STEP 2

STEP 3

STEP 4

SPAGHETTI BOLOGNESE

This familiar meat sauce, known as ragù, may also be used in lasagne, and in other baked dishes. It is so versatile that it is a good idea to make it in large quantities, and freeze some.

SERVES 4

400 g/14 oz spaghetti
1 tbsp olive oil
salt
15 g/¹/₂ oz butter
2 tbsp chopped parsley, to garnish

RAGU SAUCE:
3 tbsp olive oil
45 g/1¹/₂ oz butter
2 large onions, chopped
4 celery stalks, thinly sliced
175 g/6 oz streaky bacon, chopped into
    small strips
2 garlic cloves, chopped
500 g/1 lb lean minced beef
2 tbsp tomato purée (paste)
1 tbsp flour
1 x 425 g/15 oz can chopped tomatoes
150 ml/¹/₄ pint/²/₃ cup beef stock
150 ml/¹/₄ pint/²/₃ cup red wine
2 tsp dried oregano
¹/₂ tsp grated nutmeg
salt and pepper

1 To make the Ragu sauce: heat the oil and the butter in a large frying pan over a medium heat. Add the onions, celery and bacon pieces and fry them together for 5 minutes, stirring once or twice.

2 Stir in the garlic and minced beef and cook, stirring, until the meat has lost its redness. Lower the heat and continue cooking for a further 10 minutes, stirring once or twice.

3 Increase the heat to medium, stir in the tomato purée (paste) and the flour and cook for 1-2 minutes. Stir in the chopped tomatoes and the beef stock and wine and bring to the boil, stirring. Season the sauce and stir in the oregano and nutmeg. Cover the pan and simmer for 45 minutes, stirring occasionally.

4 Cook the spaghetti in a large pan of boiling salted water, adding the olive oil. When it is almost tender, drain in a colander, then return to the pan. Dot the spaghetti with the butter and toss thoroughly.

5 Taste the sauce and adjust the seasoning if necessary. Pour the sauce over the spaghetti and toss well. Sprinkle on the parsley to garnish and serve immediately.

STUFFED CANNELONI

Cannelloni, the thick round pasta tubes, make perfect containers for close-textured sauces of all kinds.

STEP 1

STEP 2

STEP 4

STEP 5

SERVES 4
OVEN: 190°C/375°F/GAS 5

8 cannelloni tubes
1 tbsp olive oil
fresh herbs, to garnish

FILLING:
30 g/1 oz/2 tbsp butter
300 g/10 oz frozen spinach, defrosted and
    chopped
125 g/4 oz /¹/₂ cup Ricotta
30 g/1 oz/¹/₄ cup grated Parmesan
60 g/2 oz/¹/₄ cup chopped ham
¹/₄ tsp grated nutmeg
2 tbsp double (heavy) cream
2 eggs, lightly beaten
salt and pepper

SAUCE:
30 g/1 oz/2 tbsp butter
30 g/1 oz/¹/₄ cup flour
300 ml/¹/₂ pint/1¹/₄ cups milk
2 bay leaves
large pinch of grated nutmeg
30 g/1 oz /¹/₄ cup grated Parmesan

1 To prepare the filling, melt the butter in a pan and stir in the spinach. Stir for 2-3 minutes to allow the moisture to evaporate, then remove the pan from the heat. Stir in the cheeses and the ham. Season with nutmeg, salt and pepper and beat in the cream and eggs to make a thick paste. Set aside to cool.

2 Cook the cannelloni in a large pan of boiling salted water, adding the olive oil. When almost tender, after 10-12 minutes, drain in a colander and set aside to cool.

3 To make the sauce, melt the butter in a pan, stir in the flour and, when it has formed a roux, gradually pour on the milk, stirring all the time. Add the bay leaves, bring to simmering point, and cook for 5 minutes. Season with nutmeg, salt and pepper. Remove the pan from the heat and discard the bay leaves.

4 To assemble the dish, spoon the filling into a piping bag and pipe it into each of the cannelloni tubes.

5 Spoon a little of the sauce into a shallow baking dish. Arrange the cannelloni in a single layer, then pour over the remaining sauce. Sprinkle on the remaining Parmesan cheese and bake in the preheated oven for 40-45 minutes, until the sauce is golden brown and bubbling. Serve garnished with fresh herb sprigs.

LASAGNE VERDE

*The sauce in this delicious baked pasta dish is the same sauce
that is served with Spaghetti Bolognese (page 24).*

STEP 2

SERVES 6

OVEN 190°C/375°F/GAS 5

Ragù Sauce (see page 24)
1 tbsp olive oil
250 g/8 oz lasagne verde
60 g/2 oz/$\frac{1}{2}$ cup Parmesan, grated
Bechamel sauce (see page 78)
salt and pepper
green salad, tomato salad or black olives,
*   to serve*

1 Begin by making the Ragù Sauce
as described on page 24. Cook the
sauce for 10-12 minutes longer than
the time given, in an uncovered pan, to
allow the excess liquid to evaporate. To
layer the sauce with lasagne, it needs
to be reduced in this way until it has
the consistency of a thick paste.

2 Have ready a large pan of boiling,
salted water and add the olive oil.
Drop the pasta sheets into the boiling
water 2 or 3 at a time, and return the
water to the boil before adding further
pasta sheets. If you are using fresh
lasagne, cook the sheets for a total of
8 minutes. If you are using dried or
partly precooked pasta, cook it
according to the directions given on the
packet.

3 Spread a large, dampened tea towel
on the working surface. Lift out the
pasta sheets with a slotted spoon and
spread them in a single layer on the tea
towel. Use a second tea towel if
necessary. Set the pasta aside while you
make the Bechamel sauce, as described
on page 78.

STEP 3

4 Grease a rectangular ovenproof
dish, about 25-28 cm/10-11 in
long. To assemble the dish, spoon a little
of the meat sauce into the prepared dish,
cover with a layer of lasagne, then spoon
over a little Bechamel sauce and sprinkle
on a little cheese. Continue making
layers in this way, covering the final
layer of lasagne with the remaining
Bechamel sauce.

STEP 4a

5 Sprinkle on the remaining cheese
and bake in the preheated oven for
40 minutes, until the sauce is golden
brown and bubbling. Serve with a chilled
green salad, a tomato salad, or a bowl of
black olives.

STEP 4b

TAGLIATELLE WITH CHICKEN

Spinach ribbon noodles covered with a rich tomato sauce and topped with creamy chicken makes a very appetizing dish.

STEP 1a

STEP 1b

STEP 2

STEP 3

SERVES 4

250 g/8 oz fresh green ribbon noodles
1 tbsp olive oil
salt
basil leaves, to garnish
Tomato Sauce (see page 77)

CHICKEN SAUCE:
60 g/2 oz/¼ cup unsalted butter
400 g/14 oz boned, skinned chicken breast,
   thinly sliced
90 g/3 oz/¾ cup blanched almonds
300 ml/½ pint/1¼ cups double (heavy)
   cream
salt and pepper
basil leaves, to garnish

1 Make the Tomato Sauce, as described on page 77, and keep warm.

2 To make the Chicken Sauce, melt the butter in a pan over a medium heat and fry the chicken strips and almonds for 5-6 minutes, stirring frequently, until the chicken is cooked through.

3 Meanwhile, pour the cream into a small pan over a low heat, bring it to the boil and boil for about 10 minutes, until reduced by almost half. Pour the cream over the chicken and almonds, stir well, and season. Set it aside and keep it warm.

4 Cook the fresh pasta in a large pan of boiling salted water, first adding the oil. When the pasta is just tender, about 5 minutes, drain in a colander, then return it to the pan, cover and keep it warm.

5 To assemble the dish, turn the pasta into a warmed serving dish and spoon the tomato sauce over it. Spoon the chicken and cream over the centre, scatter the basil leaves over and serve at once.

TOMATO SAUCE

This tomato sauce (see recipe on page 77) can be served with a variety of pasta dishes. Make double quantities and keep some in the freezer as a useful standby for quick and easy pasta dishes.

STEP 2

STEP 5a

STEP 5b

STEP 6

LAYERED MEAT LOAF

The cheesy pasta layer comes as a pleasant surprise inside this lightly spiced meat loaf.

SERVES 6
OVEN: 180°C/350°F/GAS 4

30 g/1 oz/2 tbsp butter, plus extra for
   greasing
1 onion, finely chopped
1 small red (bell) pepper, cored, seeded and
   chopped
1 garlic clove, chopped
500 g/1 lb lean beef, minced
30 g/1 oz/½ cup soft white breadcrumbs
½ tsp cayenne pepper
1 tbsp lemon juice
½ tsp grated lemon rind
2 tbsp chopped parsley
4 bay leaves
90 g/3 oz short pasta, such as fusilli
175 g/6 oz streaky bacon rashers, rind
   removed
1 tbsp olive oil
Cheese Sauce (see page 78)
salt and pepper
salad leaves, to garnish

1 Melt the butter in a pan over a
medium heat and fry the onion and
pepper for about 3 minutes, until the
onion is translucent. Stir in the garlic
and cook it for a further 1 minute.

2 Put the meat into a large bowl and
mash it with a wooden spoon until
it becomes a sticky paste. Tip in the fried
vegetables and stir in the breadcrumbs,
cayenne, lemon juice, lemon rind and
parsley. Season the mixture with salt and
pepper and set it aside.

3 Cook the pasta in a large pan of
boiling water to which you have
added salt and the olive oil. When it is
almost tender, drain in a colander.

4 Make the Cheese Sauce (see page
78). Stir in the pasta.

5 Grease a 1 kg/2 lb loaf tin and
arrange the bay leaves in the base.
Stretch the bacon rashers with the back
of a knife blade and arrange them to line
the base and the sides of the tin. Spoon in
half the meat mixture, level the surface
and cover it with the pasta. Spoon in the
remaining meat mixture, level the top
and cover the tin with foil.

6 Cook the meat loaf in the preheated
oven for 1 hour, or until the juices
run clear and the loaf has shrunk away
from the sides of the tin. Pour off any
excess fat from the tin and turn the loaf
out on a warmed serving dish, loosening
the edges if necessary. Serve hot, with a
green salad.

STEP 2

STEP 3

STEP 5

STEP 6

AUBERGINE (EGGPLANT) CAKE

Layers of toasty-brown aubergines, meat sauce and cheese-flavoured pasta make this a popular family supper dish.

SERVES 4
OVEN: 190°C/375°F/GAS 5

1 medium aubergine (eggplant), thinly sliced
5 tbsp olive oil
250 g/8 oz short pasta shapes, such as fusilli
60 g/2 oz/¹⁄₄ cup butter, plus extra for greasing
45 g/1¹⁄₂ oz/6 tbsp flour
300 ml/¹⁄₂ pint/1¹⁄₄ cups milk
150ml/¹⁄₄ pint/²⁄₃ cup single cream
150 ml/¹⁄₄ pint/²⁄₃ cup chicken stock
large pinch of grated nutmeg
90 g/3 oz/³⁄₄ cup Cheddar cheese, grated
Lamb Sauce (see page 79)
30 g/1 oz/¹⁄₄ cup Parmesan, grated
artichoke heart and tomato salad, to serve

1 Put the aubergine (eggplant) slices in a colander, sprinkle with salt and leave for about 45 minutes, while the salt draws out some of the bitter juices. Rinse the aubergines (eggplant) under cold, running water and drain. Toss them in paper towels to dry.

2 Heat 4 tablespoons of the oil in a frying pan over a medium heat. Fry the aubergine (eggplant) slices for about 4 minutes on each side, until they are light golden brown. Remove with a slotted spoon and drain on paper towels.

3 Make the Lamb Sauce as described on page 79 and keep warm.

4 Meanwhile, cook the pasta in a large pan of boiling salted water, adding 1 tablespoon of olive oil. When the pasta is almost tender, drain it in a colander and return to the pan. Cover and keep warm.

5 Melt the butter in a small pan, stir in the flour and cook for 1 minute. Gradually pour on the milk, stirring all the time, then stir in the cream and chicken stock. Season with nutmeg, salt and pepper, bring to the boil and simmer for 5 minutes. Stir in the Cheddar cheese and remove from the heat. Pour half the sauce over the pasta and mix well. Reserve the remaining sauce.

6 Grease a shallow ovenproof dish. Spoon in half the pasta, cover it with half the meat sauce and then with the aubergines (eggplant) in a single layer. Repeat the layers of pasta and meat sauce and spread the remaining cheese sauce over the top. Sprinkle on the Parmesan cheese. Bake in the preheated oven for 25 minutes, until the top is golden brown. Serve hot or cold, with artichoke heart salad.

PASTICCIO

A recipe that has both Italian and Greek origins, this dish may be served hot or cold, cut into thick, satisfying squares.

STEP 1

SERVES 6
OVEN: 190°C/375°F/GAS 5

250 g/8 oz fusilli, or other short pasta
  shapes
1 tbsp olive oil
4 tbsp double(heavy) cream
salt
rosemary sprigs, to garnish

SAUCE:
2 tbsp olive oil, plus extra for brushing
1 onion, thinly sliced
1 red (bell) pepper, cored, seeded and chopped
2 cloves garlic, chopped
625 g/1¼ lb lean beef, minced
1 x 425 g/15 oz can chopped tomatoes
125 ml/4 fl oz/½ cup dry white wine
2 tbsp chopped parsley
1 x 50 g/2 oz can anchovies, drained and
  chopped
salt and pepper

TOPPING:
300 ml/½ pint/1¼ cups plain yogurt
3 eggs
pinch of nutmeg
45 g/1½ oz/ ⅓ cup Parmesan, grated

1 To make the sauce, heat the oil in a large frying pan and fry the onion and red (bell) pepper for 3 minutes. Stir in the garlic and cook for 1 minute more. Stir in the beef and cook, stirring frequently, until it has changed colour.

2 Add the tomatoes and wine, stir well and bring to the boil. Simmer, uncovered, for 20 minutes, until the sauce is fairly thick. Stir in the parsley and anchovies and adjust the seasoning.

3 Cook the pasta in a large pan of boiling salted water, adding the oil. When it is almost tender, drain it in a colander, then transfer it to a bowl. Stir in the cream and set it aside.

4 To make the topping, beat together the yogurt and eggs and season the mixture with nutmeg, salt and pepper. Stir in the cheese.

5 Brush a shallow baking dish with oil. Spoon in half the macaroni and cover with half of the meat sauce. Repeat these layers, spread the topping evenly over the dish and sprinkle on the cheese.

6 Bake in the preheated oven for 25 minutes, until the topping is golden brown and bubbling. Garnish with rosemary and serve with a selection of raw vegetable crudités.

STEP 2

STEP 4

STEP 5

TAGLIATELLI WITH MEATBALLS

There is an appetizing contrast of textures and flavours in this satisfying family dish.

STEP 1

STEP 2a

STEP 2b

STEP 3

SERVES 4

500 g/1 lb lean minced beef
60 g/2 oz/1 cup soft white breadcrumbs
1 garlic clove, crushed
2 tbsp chopped parsley
1 tsp dried oregano
large pinch of grated nutmeg
1/4 tsp ground coriander
60 g/2 oz/1/2 cup Parmesan, grated
2-3 tbsp milk
flour, for dusting
4 tbsp olive oil
400 g/14 oz tagliatelli
30 g/1 oz/2 tbsp butter, diced
salt
2 tbsp chopped parsley, to garnish

SAUCE:
3 tbsp olive oil
2 large onions, sliced
2 celery stalks, thinly sliced
2 garlic cloves, chopped
1 x 425 g/15 oz can chopped tomatoes
125 g/4 oz bottled sun-dried tomatoes,
    drained and chopped
2 tbsp tomato purée (paste)
1 tbsp dark Muscovado sugar
150 ml/1/4 pint/2/3 cup white wine, or water
salt and pepper
green salad, to serve

1 To make the sauce, heat the oil in a frying pan and fry the onion and celery until translucent. Add the garlic and cook for 1 minute. Stir in the tomatoes, tomato purée (paste), sugar and wine and season. Bring to the boil and simmer for 10 minutes.

2 Break up the meat in a bowl with a wooden spoon until it becomes a sticky paste. Stir in the breadcrumbs, garlic, herbs and spices. Stir in the cheese and enough milk to make a firm paste. Flour your hands, take large spoonfuls of the mixture and shape it into 12 balls. Heat the oil in a frying pan and fry the meatballs for 5-6 minutes until browned.

3 Pour the tomato sauce over the meatballs. Lower the heat, cover the pan and simmer for 30 minutes, turning once or twice. Add a little extra water if the sauce begins to dry.

4 Cook the pasta in a large saucepan of boiling salted water, adding the remaining oil. When almost tender, drain in a colander, then turn into a warmed serving dish, dot with the butter and toss with 2 forks. Spoon the meatballs and sauce over the pasta and sprinkle on the parsley. Serve with a green salad.

CHAPTER THREE

Pasta with Fish Sauces

Macaroni with mushrooms and prawns (shrimp) or calamares; wholewheat lasagne with smoked fish and prawns (shrimp); pasta shells with mussels; spaghetti with smoked salmon or with anchovies and tuna; vermicelli with clams – these are irresistible combinations that have a whiff of the sea and, in most cases, the flavour of the Mediterranean.

These dishes are as practical as they are delicious, all perfect choices for the busy cook who has to keep an eye on the clock. In general, since fish and seafood needs only the briefest of cooking times, the sauce and the pasta can be ready together, perfectly cooked and perfectly timed just as the family is assembling or the guests are arriving.

Opposite: *Open-air restaurant beside Lake Garda. The many rivers and lakes in Italy are a rich source of fish and shellfish, which feature largely in pasta sauces.*

SPAGHETTI WITH SEAFOOD SAUCE

A packet of prawns (shrimp) in the freezer can become the star ingredient in this colourful and tasty dish.

STEP 2

SERVES 4

250 g/8 oz short-cut spaghetti, or long
   spaghetti broken into 15 cm/6 in lengths
2 tbsp olive oil
300 ml/¹/₂ pint/1¹/₄ cups chicken stock
1 tsp lemon juice
1 small cauliflower, cut into florets
2 medium carrots, thinly sliced
125 g/4 oz mangetout (snow peas),
   trimmed
60 g/2 oz/¹/₄ cup butter
1 onion, sliced
250 g/8 oz courgettes (zucchini), thinly
   sliced
1 garlic clove, chopped
350 g/12 oz frozen shelled prawns
   (shrimp), defrosted
2 tbsp chopped parsley
30 g/1 oz/¹/₄ cup Parmesan, grated
salt and pepper
¹/₂ tsp paprika, to sprinkle
4 unshelled prawns (shrimp), to garnish
   (optional)

1 Cook the spaghetti in a large pan of boiling salted water, adding 1 tablespoon of the olive oil. When it is almost tender, drain in a colander. Return to the pan and stir in the remaining olive oil. Cover the pan and keep warm.

2 Bring the chicken stock and lemon juice to the boil in a pan over medium heat and cook the cauliflower and carrots for 3-4 minutes, until they are barely tender. Remove with a slotted spoon and set aside. Add the mangetout (snow peas) to the stock and cook for 3-4 minutes, until they begin to soften. Remove with a slotted spoon and add to the other vegetables. Reserve the stock for future use.

3 Melt half the butter in a frying pan over medium heat and fry the onion and courgettes (zucchini) for about 3 minutes. Add the garlic and prawns (shrimp) and cook for a further 2-3 minutes, until they are thoroughly heated through.

4 Stir in the reserved vegetables and season well. When the vegetables are heated through stir in the remaining butter.

5 Transfer the spaghetti to a warmed serving dish. Pour on the sauce and parsley and toss well, using 2 forks, until thoroughly coated. Sprinkle on the grated cheese and paprika and garnish with prawns (shrimp), if using. Serve immediately.

STEP 3a

STEP 3b

STEP 4

43

STEP 2

STEP 3

STEP 4a

STEP 4b

MACARONI & PRAWN (SHRIMP)

This adaptation of an 18th-century Italian dish is baked until it is golden brown and sizzling, then cut into wedges, like a cake.

SERVES 4
OVEN: 180°C/350°F/GAS 4

350 g/12 oz short pasta, such as short-cut macaroni
1 tbsp olive oil, plus extra for brushing
90 g/3 oz/6 tbsp butter, plus extra for greasing
2 small fennel bulbs, thinly sliced, leaves reserved
175 g/6 oz mushrooms, thinly sliced
175 g/6 oz shelled prawns (shrimp)
60 g/2 oz/½ cup Parmesan, grated
2 large tomatoes, sliced
1 tsp dried oregano
salt and pepper
Bechamel Sauce (see page 78)
pinch of cayenne

1 Cook the pasta in a large pan of boiling, salted water to which you have added 1 tablespoon of olive oil. When the pasta is almost tender, drain it in a colander, return to the pan and dot with 30g/1 oz/2 tablespoons of the butter. Shake the pan well, cover and keep the pasta warm.

2 Melt the remaining butter in a pan over medium heat and fry the fennel for 3-4 minutes, until it begins to soften. Stir in the mushrooms and fry for a further 2 minutes. Stir in the prawns (shrimp), remove the pan from the heat and set it aside.

3 Make the Bechamel Sauce and add the cayenne. Remove the pan from the heat and stir in the reserved vegetables, prawns (shrimp) and the pasta.

4 Grease a round, shallow baking dish. Pour in the pasta mixture and spread evenly. Sprinkle on the Parmesan, and arrange the tomato slices in a ring around the edge of the dish. Brush the tomato with olive oil and sprinkle on the dried oregano.

5 Bake in the preheated oven for 25 minutes, until the top is golden brown. Serve hot.

ACCOMPANIMENT

A mixed green salad, tossed with the reserved fennel leaves and sprinkled with crumbled feta cheese, goes well with this dish.

SEAFOOD LASAGNE

Layers of cheese sauce, smoked cod and wholewheat lasagne can be assembled overnight and left ready to cook on the following day.

SERVES 6
OVEN: 190°C/375°F/GAS 5

8 sheets wholewheat lasagne
500 g/1 lb smoked cod
600 ml/1 pint/2¹⁄₂ cups milk
1 tbsp lemon juice
8 peppercorns
2 bay leaves
a few stalks of parsley
60 g/2 oz/¹⁄₂ cup Cheddar, grated
30 g/1 oz/¹⁄₄ cup Parmesan, grated
salt and pepper
a few whole prawns (shrimp), to garnish
    (optional)

SAUCE:
60 g/2 oz/¹⁄₄ cup butter, plus extra for
    greasing
1 large onion, sliced
1 green (bell) pepper, cored, seeded,and
    chopped
1 small courgette (zucchini), sliced
60 g/2 oz/¹⁄₂ cup flour
150 ml/¹⁄₄ pint/²⁄₃ cup white wine
150 ml/¹⁄₄ pint/²⁄₃ cup single cream
125 g/4 oz shelled prawns(shrimp)
60 g/2 oz/¹⁄₂ cup Cheddar, grated

1 Cook the lasagne in boiling, salted water until almost tender, as described on page 29. Drain and reserve.

2 Place the smoked cod, milk, lemon juice, peppercorns, bay leaves and parsley in a frying pan. Bring to the boil, cover and simmer for 10 minutes.

STEP 2

3 Remove the fish, skin and remove any bones. Flake the fish. Strain and reserve the liquor.

4 Make the sauce: melt the butter in a pan and fry the onion, (bell) pepper and courgette (zucchini) for 2-3 minutes. Stir in the flour and cook for 1 minute. Gradually add the fish liquor, then stir in the wine, cream and prawns (shrimp). Simmer for 2 minutes. Remove from the heat, add the cheese, and season.

STEP 4

5 Grease a shallow baking dish. Pour in a quarter of the sauce and spread evenly over the base. Cover the sauce with 3 sheets of lasagne, then with another quarter of the sauce. Arrange the fish on top, then cover with half the remaining sauce. Finish with the remaining lasagne, then the rest of the sauce. Sprinkle the Cheddar and Parmesan over the sauce.

STEP 5a

6 Bake in the preheated oven for 25 minutes, or until the top is golden brown and bubbling. Garnish with a few whole prawns (shrimp), if liked.

STEP 5b

PASTA SHELLS WITH MUSSELS

*Serve this aromatic seafood dish to family and friends
who admit to a love of garlic!*

STEP 1

STEP 2

STEP 3

STEP 5

SERVES 4-6

400 g/14 oz pasta shells
1 tbsp olive oil

SAUCE:
3.5 litres/6 pints mussels, scrubbed
2 large onions, chopped
250 ml/8 fl oz/1 cup dry white wine
125 g/4 oz/¹/₂ cup unsalted butter
6 large garlic cloves, finely chopped
5 tbsp chopped parsley
*300 ml/¹/₂ pint/1¹/₄ cup double (heavy)
   cream*
salt and pepper
crusty bread, to serve

1 Pull off the "beards" from the mussels and rinse well in several changes of water. Discard any mussels that refuse to close when tapped. Put the mussels in a large pan with one of the onions and the white wine. Cover the pan, shake and cook over a medium heat for 2-3 minutes until they open.

2 Remove the pan from the heat, lift out the mussels with a slotted spoon, reserving the liquor, and set aside until they are cool enough to handle. Discard any mussels that have not opened.

3 Melt the butter in a pan over medium heat and fry the remaining onion until translucent. Stir in the garlic and cook for 1 further minute. Gradually pour on the reserved cooking liquor, stirring to blend thoroughly. Stir in the parsley and cream, season and bring to simmering point. Taste and adjust the seasoning if necessary.

4 Cook the pasta in a large pan of salted boiling water, adding the oil. When it is almost tender, drain in a colander. Return the pasta to the pan, cover and keep warm.

5 Remove the mussels from their shells, reserving a few for garnish. Stir the mussels into the cream sauce. Tip the pasta into a warmed serving dish, pour on the sauce and, using 2 large spoons, toss it well. Garnish with a few mussel shells. Serve hot, with warm, crusty bread.

PASTA SHELLS

Pasta shells, from medium-sized to giant ones, are ideal for this dish, because the rich, buttery sauce collects in the cavities and impregnates the pasta with the flavours of the shellfish and wine.

STEP 1

STEP 2

STEP 3a

STEP 3b

SPAGHETTI WITH SMOKED SALMON

Made in moments, this is a dish to astonish and delight unexpected guests.

SERVES 4

500 g / 1 lb buckwheat spaghetti
2 tbsp olive oil
90 g / 3 oz / $^{1}/_{2}$ cup feta cheese, crumbled

SAUCE:
300 ml / $^{1}/_{2}$ pint / $1^{1}/_{4}$ cups double (heavy) cream
150 ml / $^{1}/_{4}$ pint / $^{2}/_{3}$ cup whisky or brandy
125 g / 4 oz smoked salmon
large pinch of cayenne pepper
2 tbsp chopped coriander, or parsley
salt and pepper

1 Cook the spaghetti in a large pan of salted boiling water, adding 1 tablespoon of the olive oil. When the pasta is almost tender, drain it in a colander. Return to the pan and sprinkle on the remaining oil. Cover and shake the pan and keep warm.

2 In separate small pans, heat the cream and the whisky or brandy to simmering point, but do not let it boil

3 Combine the cream and whisky or brandy. Cut the smoked salmon into thin strips and add to the cream. Season with pepper and cayenne, and stir in the chopped herb.

4 Transfer the spaghetti to a warmed serving dish, pour on the sauce and toss thoroughly using 2 large forks. Scatter the crumbled cheese over the pasta and garnish with coriander leaves. Serve at once.

ACCOMPANIMENTS

A green salad with a lemony dressing is a good accompaniment to this rich and luxurious dish.

VERMICELLI WITH CLAM SAUCE

*Another cook-in-a-hurry recipe that transforms storecupboard
ingredients into a dish with style.*

STEP 1

SERVES 4

400 g/14 oz vermicelli, spaghetti, or other
   long pasta
1 tbsp olive oil
30 g/1 oz/2 tbsp butter
2 tbsp flaked Parmesan, to garnish
sprig of basil, to garnish

SAUCE:

1 tbsp olive oil
2 onions, chopped
2 garlic cloves, chopped
2 x 200 g/7 oz jars clams in brine
125 ml/4 fl oz/½ cup white wine
4 tbsp chopped parsley
½ tsp dried oregano
pinch of grated nutmeg
salt and pepper

1 Cook the pasta in a large pan of
boiling salted water, adding the
olive oil. When it is almost tender, drain
in a colander, return to the pan and add
the butter. Cover the pan. Shake it and
keep it warm.

2 To make the clam sauce, heat the
oil in a pan over a medium heat
and fry the onion until it is translucent.
Stir in the garlic and cook for 1 further
minute.

3 Strain the liquid from one jar of
clams, pour into the pan and add
the wine. Stir well, bring to simmering
point and simmer for 3 minutes. Drain
the brine from the second jar of clams
and discard. Add the shellfish and herbs
to the pan and season with pepper and
nutmeg. Lower the heat and cook until
the sauce is heated through.

4 Transfer the pasta to a warmed
serving dish, and pour on the
sauce. Sprinkle on the Parmesan and
garnish with the basil. Serve hot.

STEP 2

STEP 3a

PARMESAN

You could use grated Parmesan for this
dish, but flakes of fresh Parmesan, carved
off the block, will give it an added depth of
flavour.

STEP 3b

STEP 2a

STEP 2b

STEP 3a

STEP 3b

SPAGHETTI WITH TUNA & PARSLEY

This is a recipe to look forward to when parsley is at its most prolific, in the growing season.

SERVES 4

500 g/1 lb spaghetti
1 tbsp olive oil
30 g/1 oz/2 tbsp butter
black olives, to garnish

SAUCE:
1 x 200 g/7 oz can tuna, drained
1 x 50 g/2 oz can anchovies, drained
250 ml/8 fl oz/1 cup olive oil
1 cup roughly chopped parsley
150 ml/^{1}/$_4$ pint/^{2}/$_3$ cup crème fraîche
salt and pepper

1 Cook the spaghetti in a large pan of salted boiling water, adding the olive oil. When it is almost tender, drain in a colander and return to the pan. Add the butter, toss thoroughly to coat and keep warm.

2 Remove any bones from the tuna. Put it into a blender or food processor with the anchovies, olive oil and parsley and process until the sauce is smooth. Pour on the crème fraîche and process for a few seconds to blend. Taste the sauce and season

3 Warm 4 plates. Shake the pan of spaghetti over medium heat until it is thoroughly warmed through. Pour on the sauce and toss quickly, using 2 forks. Garnish with the olives and serve immediately with warm, crusty bread.

KNOW YOUR OIL

Oils produced by different countries, mainly Italy, Spain and Greece, have their own characteristic flavours. Some olive varieties produce an oil which has a hot and peppery taste, while others, such as the Kalamata, grown in Greece, give a distinctly "green" flavour. Get to know and recognise the different grades of oil, too. Extra virgin olive oil, the finest grade, is made from the first, cold pressing of olives. Virgin olive oil, which has a fine aroma and colour, is also made by cold pressing. It may have a slightly higher acidity level than extra virgin oil. Refined or pure olive oil is made by treating the paste residue with heat or solvents to remove the residual oil. Olive oil is a blend of refined and virgin olive oil.

STEP 2

STEP 3a

STEP 3b

STEP 5

NORTH SEA PASTA PUDDING

A tasty mixture of creamy fish and pasta cooked in a bowl, unmoulded and drizzled with tomato sauce presents macaroni in a new guise.

SERVES 4

125 g/4 oz short-cut macaroni, or other
    short pasta shapes
1 tbsp olive oil
15 g/¹/₂ oz/1 tbsp butter, plus extra for
    greasing
500 g/1 lb white fish fillets, such as cod,
    haddock or coley
a few parsley stalks
6 black peppercorns
125 ml/4 oz/¹/₂ cup double (heavy) cream
2 eggs, separated
2 tbsp chopped dill, or parsley
freshly ground black pepper
pinch of grated nutmeg
60 g/2 oz/¹/₂ cup Parmesan, grated
Tomato Sauce (see page 77), to serve
dill or parsley sprigs, to garnish

1 Cook the pasta in a large pan of salted boiling water, adding the oil. Drain in a colander, add the butter and cover the pan. Keep the pasta warm.

2 Place the fish in a frying pan with the parsley stalks and peppercorns and pour on just enough water to cover. Bring to the boil, cover and simmer for 10 minutes. Lift out the fish with a fish slice, reserving the liquor. When the fish is cool enough to handle, skin and remove any remaining bones. Cut into bite-sized pieces.

3 Transfer the pasta to a large bowl and stir in the cream, egg yolks and dill. Stir in the fish, taking care not to break it up, and enough liquor to make a moist but firm mixture. It should fall easily from a spoon but not be too runny. Whisk the egg whites until stiff but not dry, then fold into the mixture.

4 Grease a heatproof bowl or pudding basin and spoon in the mixture to within 4 cm/1½ in of the rim. Cover the top with greased greaseproof paper and a cloth, or with foil, and tie firmly around the rim. Do not use foil if you cook the pudding in a microwave.

5 Stand the pudding on a trivet in a large pan of boiling water to come halfway up the sides. Cover and steam for 1½ hours, topping up the boiling water as needed, or cook in a microwave on maximum power for 7 minutes.

6 Run a knife around the inside of the bowl and invert on to a warmed serving dish. Pour some tomato sauce over the top and serve the rest separately. Garnish with the herb sprigs.

STEP 2a

STEP 2b

STEP 3

STEP 4

CALAMARES AND MACARONI

This Greek dish is quick and easy to make, yet has all the authentic flavour of the islands.

SERVES 4-6

250 g/8 oz short-cut macaroni, or other
   short pasta shapes
1 tbsp olive oil
2 tbsp chopped parsley
salt and pepper

SAUCE:
350 g/12 oz cleaned squid
6 tbsp olive oil
2 onions, sliced
150 ml/¼ pint/⅔ cup red wine
250 ml/8 fl oz/1 cup fish stock
350 g/12 oz tomatoes, skinned and thinly
   sliced
2 tbsp tomato purée (paste)
1 tsp dried oregano
2 bay leaves

1 Cook the pasta for only 3 minutes in a large pan of boiling salted water, adding the oil. When it is almost tender, drain the pasta in a colander, return to the pan, cover and keep warm.

2 Cut the squid into 4 cm/1½ in strips. Heat the oil in a pan over medium heat and fry the onion until translucent. Add the squid and stock and simmer for 5 minutes. Pour on the wine and add the tomatoes, tomato purée

(paste), oregano and bay leaves. Bring the sauce to the boil, season and cook, uncovered, for 5 minutes.

3 Add the pasta, stir well, cover the pan and continue simmering it for 10 minutes, or until the macaroni and squid is almost tender. By this time the sauce should be thick and syrupy. If it is too liquid uncover the pan and continue cooking for a few minutes. Taste the sauce and adjust the seasoning if necessary.

4 Remove the bay leaves and stir in most of the parsley, reserving a little to garnish. Transfer to a warmed serving dish. Sprinkle on the remaining parsley and serve hot. Serve with warm, crusty bread such as ciabatta.

CLEANING SQUID

Peel off the skin and cut off the head and tentacles. Remove the transparent bone from the body then turn the body sac inside out and wash thoroughly. Cut off the tentacles to use and discard the head.

CHAPTER FOUR

Pasta & Vegetable Dishes

Aubergine (eggplant) shells filled with Mozzarella cheese and pasta
shapes; crisp and crunchy vegetables like celery and
(bell) peppers stir-fried with pasta shells and tossed in a sweet
and sour sauce; a Spanish pasta omelette of just-cooked eggs
flavoured with onion, fennel and garlic – this section
takes you on a gastronomic tour
around the world.

Whether you choose to simmer vegetables lightly in water or stock,
to steam them or to stir-fry them, be sure to cook them only until
they, like the pasta, are al dente and still slightly crisp.
In this way the vegetables will retain more of their nutrients
and most of their colour and will contrast both
appealingly and deliciously with
their pasta accompaniment.

Opposite: *The rolling hills of
Val d'Oreia, near Pienza,
Tuscany. Much of the country's
food – grains, rice, meat, fruit
and vegetables – is produced in
the fertile Tuscan soil.*

PASTA WITH GREEN VEGETABLES

The different shapes and textures of the vegetables make a mouthwatering presentation in this light and summery dish.

STEP 2a

STEP 2b

STEP 4a

STEP 4b

SERVES 4

250 g/8 oz gemelli or other pasta shapes
1 tbsp olive oil
2 tbsp chopped parsley
salt and pepper

SAUCE:
1 head green broccoli, cut into florets
2 medium courgettes (zucchini), sliced
250 g/8 oz asparagus spears, trimmed
125 g/4 oz mangetout (snow peas),
  trimmed
125 g/4 oz frozen peas
30 g/1 oz/2 tbsp butter
3 tbsp vegetable stock
5 tbsp double (heavy) cream
large pinch of grated nutmeg
2 tbsp grated Parmesan

1 Cook the pasta in a large pan of salted boiling water, adding the olive oil. When almost tender, drain the pasta in a colander and return to the pan, cover and keep warm.

2 Steam the broccoli, courgettes (zucchini), asparagus spears and mangetout (snow peas) over a pan of boiling, salted water until they are just beginning to soften. Remove from the heat and plunge into cold water to prevent them from cooking further in the residual heat. Drain and set them aside.

3 Cook the frozen peas in boiling, salted water for 3 minutes, then drain. Refresh in cold water and drain again.

4 Put the butter and vegetable stock in a pan over a medium heat. Add all the vegetables except the asparagus spears and toss carefully with a wooden spoon to heat through, taking care not to break them up. Stir in the cream, allow the sauce just to heat through and season well with salt, pepper and nutmeg.

5 Transfer the pasta to a warmed serving dish and stir in the chopped parsley. Spoon the sauce over, and sprinkle on the Parmesan. Arrange the asparagus spears in a pattern on top. Serve hot.

STEP 1

STEP 3

STEP 5a

STEP 5b

VEGETARIAN CASSOULET

A satisfying winter dish, this vegetable and pasta cassoulet is derived from the slow-cooked, one-pot meals of the Languedoc, in the south of France.

SERVES 6
OVEN: 180°C/350°F/Gas 4

250 g/8 oz/generous 1 cup dried haricot
  beans, soaked and drained
250 g/8 oz penne, or other short pasta
  shapes
6 tbsp olive oil
900 ml/1¹/₂ pints/3¹/₂ cups vegetable stock
2 large onions, sliced
2 cloves garlic, chopped
2 bay leaves
1 tsp dried oregano
1 tsp dried thyme
5 tbsp red wine
2 tbsp tomato purée (paste)
2 celery stalks, sliced
1 fennel bulb, sliced
125 g/4 oz mushrooms, sliced
250 g/8 oz tomatoes, sliced
1 tsp dark Muscovado sugar
4 tbsp dry white breadcrumbs
salt and pepper
salad leaves and crusty bread, to serve

1 Put the beans in a large pan, cover them with water and bring to the boil. Boil the beans rapidly for 20 minutes, then drain them.

2 Cook the pasta for only 3 minutes in a large pan of boiling salted water, adding 1 tablespoon of the oil. When almost tender, drain the pasta in a colander and set it aside.

3 Place the beans in a large flameproof casserole, pour on the vegetable stock and stir in the remaining olive oil, the onions, garlic, bay leaves, herbs, wine and tomato purée (paste).

4 Bring the stock to the boil, cover the casserole and cook it in the oven for 2 hours.

5 Add the reserved pasta, the celery, fennel, mushrooms and tomatoes, and season with salt and pepper. Stir in the sugar and sprinkle on the breadcrumbs. Cover the casserole and continue cooking it for 1 hour. Serve it hot, with salad leaves and plenty of crusty bread.

NOTE

Do not use a salted vegetable stock for the initial cooking stage of this dish, since the salt would inhibit the softening process of the beans as they gradually absorb the liquid.

STEP 2

STEP 3

STEP 4

STEP 6

VEGETABLE PASTA STIR-FRY

*Prepare all the vegetables and cook the pasta in advance,
then the dish can be cooked in a few minutes.*

SERVES 4

*400 g/14 oz wholewheat pasta shells, or
 other short pasta shapes*
1 tbsp olive oil
2 carrots, thinly sliced
125 g/4 oz baby sweetcorn
3 tbsp peanut oil
*2.5 cm/1 in ginger root, peeled and thinly
 sliced*
1 large onion, thinly sliced
1 garlic clove, thinly sliced
3 celery stalks, thinly sliced
*1 small red (bell) pepper, cored, seeded and
 sliced into matchstick strips*
*1 small green (bell) pepper, cored, seeded
 and sliced into matchstick strips*
salt

SAUCE:
1 tsp cornflour (cornstarch)
2 tbsp water
3 tbsp soy sauce
3 tbsp dry sherry
1 tsp clear honey
few drops of hot pepper sauce (optional)
steamed mangetout (snow peas), to serve

1 Cook the pasta in a large pan of
boiling salted water, adding the
tablespoon of olive oil. When almost
tender, drain the pasta in a colander,
return to the pan, cover and keep the
pasta warm.

2 Cook the sliced carrot and baby
sweetcorn in boiling, salted water
for 2 minutes, then drain in a colander,
plunge into cold water to prevent further
cooking and drain again.

3 Heat the peanut oil in a wok or a
large frying pan over medium heat
and fry the ginger for 1 minute, to
flavour the oil. Remove with a slotted
spoon and discard.

4 Add the onion, garlic, celery and
(bell) peppers to the oil and stir-fry
for 2 minutes. Add the carrots and baby
sweetcorn and stir-fry for a further 2
minutes, then stir in the reserved pasta.

5 Put the cornflour (cornstarch) into
a small bowl and gradually pour
on the water, stirring constantly. Stir in
the soy sauce, sherry and honey.

6 Pour the sauce into the pan, stir
well and cook for 2 minutes,
stirring once or twice. Taste the sauce
and season with hot pepper sauce if liked.
Serve with a steamed green vegetable
such as mangetout (snow peas).

BAKED AUBERGINES (EGGPLANT)

*Combined with tomatoes and Mozzarella cheese, pasta makes a tasty
filling for baked aubergine (eggplant) shells.*

STEP 2

SERVES 4
OVEN: 200°C/400°F/GAS 6

*250 g/8 oz penne, or other short pasta
   shapes*
4 tbsp olive oil, plus extra for brushing
2 medium aubergines (eggplant)
1 large onion, chopped
2 garlic cloves, crushed
1 x 425 g/15 oz can chopped tomatoes
2 tsp dried oregano
60 g/2 oz Mozzarella, thinly sliced
30 g/1 oz/¼ cup Parmesan, grated
2 tbsp dry breadcrumbs
salt and pepper
salad leaves, to serve

1 Cook the pasta in a large pan of salted boiling water, adding 1 tablespoon of the olive oil. When it is almost tender, drain the pasta in a colander, return to the pan, cover and keep warm.

2 Cut the aubergines (eggplant) in half lengthways. Score around the inside with a knife then scoop out the flesh with a spoon, taking care not to pierce the skin. Brush the insides of the aubergine (eggplant) shells with olive oil. Chop the aubergine (eggplant) flesh and set it aside.

3 Heat the remaining oil in a frying pan over a medium heat and fry the onion until it is translucent. Add the garlic and fry for 1 further minute. Add the chopped aubergine (eggplant) and fry for 5 minutes, stirring frequently. Add the tomatoes and oregano and season with salt and pepper. Bring to the boil and simmer for 10 minutes, or until the mixture is thick. Taste and adjust the seasoning if necessary. Remove from the heat and stir in the reserved pasta.

4 Brush a baking sheet with oil and arrange the aubergine (eggplant) shells in a single layer. Divide half the tomato mixture between the four shells. Arrange the Mozzarella on top and cover with the remaining mixture, piling it into a mound. Mix together the Parmesan and breadcrumbs, and sprinkle over the top, patting it lightly into the mixture.

5 Bake in the preheated oven for 25 minutes, until the topping is golden brown. Serve hot, with a green salad.

STEP 3

STEP 4a

STEP 4b

VERMICELLI FLAN

Lightly cooked vermicelli is pressed into a flan ring and baked with a creamy mushroom filling.

STEP 2

STEP 3

STEP 4

STEP 5

SERVES 4
OVEN: 180°C/350°F/GAS 4

250 g/8 oz vermicelli or spaghetti
30 g/1 oz/2 tbsp butter, plus extra for
  greasing
salt

SAUCE:
60 g/2 oz/¼ cup butter
1 onion, chopped
150 g/5 oz button mushrooms, trimmed
1 green (bell) pepper, cored, seeded and
  sliced into thin rings
150 ml/¼ pint/⅔ cup milk
3 eggs, lightly beaten
2 tbsp double (heavy) cream
1 tsp dried oregano
pinch of grated nutmeg
freshly ground black pepper
1 tbsp grated Parmesan
tomato and basil salad, to serve

1 Cook the pasta in a large pan of salted boiling water, adding the olive oil. When almost tender, drain in a colander. Return to the pan, add the butter and shake the pan well.

2 Grease a 20 cm/8 in loose-bottomed flan tin (pan). Press the pasta on the base and round the sides to form a case.

3 Heat the butter in a frying pan over a medium heat and fry the onion well until it is translucent. Remove with a slotted spoon and spread it in the flan base.

4 Add the mushrooms and (bell) pepper rings to the pan and turn them in the fat until they are glazed. Fry them for about 2 minutes on each side, then arrange in the flan case.

5 Beat together the milk, eggs and cream, stir in the oregano and season with nutmeg and pepper. Pour the custard mixture carefully over the vegetables and sprinkle on the cheese.

6 Bake the flan in the preheated oven for 40-45 minutes, until the filling is set. Slide the flan on to a serving plate and lift off the flan ring. Serve warm.

VARIATIONS

You can use this moist and buttery flan case with any of your favourite fillings: chopped bacon, cheese and herbs, or a mixture of diced ham and sliced mushrooms; or cooked and flaked smoked haddock with sweetcorn kernels.

STEP 3a

STEP 3b

STEP 3c

STEP 4

SPANISH OMELETTE

Use any leftover cooked pasta you may have, such as penne, short-cut macaroni or shells, to make this fluffy omelette an instant success.

SERVES 2

4 tbsp olive oil
1 small Spanish onion, chopped
1 fennel bulb, thinly sliced
125 g/4 oz raw potato, diced and dried
1 garlic clove, chopped
4 eggs
1 tbsp chopped parsley
pinch of cayenne pepper
90 g/3 oz short pasta, cooked weight
1 tbsp stuffed green olives, halved, plus extra
    to garnish
salt and pepper
marjoram sprigs, to garnish
tomato salad, to serve

1 Heat 2 tablespoons of the oil in a heavy frying pan over a low heat and fry the onion, fennel and potato for 8-10 minutes, stirring occasionally, until the potato is just tender. Do not allow it to break up. Stir in the garlic and cook for 1 further minute. Remove the pan from the heat, lift out the vegetables with a slotted spoon and set them aside. Rinse and dry the pan.

2 Break the eggs into a bowl and beat them until they are frothy. Stir in the parsley and season with salt, pepper and cayenne.

3 Heat 1 tablespoon of the remaining oil in a pan over medium heat. Pour in half the beaten eggs, then add the cooked vegetables, the pasta and the olives. Pour on the remaining egg and cook until the sides begin to set.

4 Lift up the edges with a spatula to allow the uncooked egg to spread underneath. Continue cooking the omelette, shaking the pan occasionally, until the underside is golden brown.

5 Slide the omelette out on to a large, flat plate and wipe the pan clean with paper towels. Heat the remaining oil in the pan and invert the omelette. Cook on the other side until it is also golden brown.

6 Slide the omelette on to a warmed serving dish. Garnish with a few olives and marjoram, and serve hot, cut into wedges, with a tomato salad.

GETTING TO KNOW PASTA

BASIC PASTA DOUGH

If you get caught up in the enthusiasm of pasta making, you might like to buy a machine to roll, stretch and cut the dough. Once it is fully and evenly stretched, it is surprisingly easy to cut by hand.

SERVES 4

125 g/4 oz/1 cup strong plain
   flour, plus extra for dusting
125 g/4 oz/²/₃ cup fine semolina
1 tsp salt
2 tbsp olive oil
2 eggs
2-3 tbsp hot water

1. Sieve the flour, semolina and salt into a bowl and make a well in the centre. Pour in half the oil and add the eggs. Add 1 tablespoon of hot water and, using your fingertips, work to a smooth dough. Sprinkle on a little more water if necessary to make the dough pliable.

2. Lightly dust a board with flour, turn the dough out and knead it until it is elastic and silky. This might take 10-12 minutes. Dust the dough with more flour if your fingers become sticky.

   Alternatively, put the eggs, 1 tablespoon hot water and the oil in the bowl of a food processor and process for a few seconds.

continued opposite

Pasta means "paste" or "dough" in Italian, and many of the widely popular pasta dishes have their origins in Italy, where pasta has been produced at least as far back as the 13th century.

   Its principal ingredients are modest, though more and more types of fresh and dried pasta are coming on to the market. By far the most widely available commercial type is made from hard durum wheat, milled to form fine semolina grains and then extruded through drums fitted with specially perforated discs. The production methods may not sound inspiring, but the end product certainly is. The wide variety of these discs makes it possible to produce an estimated 600 different pasta shapes and sizes including strands and shells, twists and spirals, rings and tubes.

VARIETIES OF PASTA

You can choose pasta which is made from just the endosperm of the wheat, as most of it is, or from the whole wheat; this type contains more dietary fibre. Other basic types are made from ground buckwheat, which gives the product a greyish colour and distinctively nutty flavour that combines especially well with vegetable and herb sauces; with the addition of spinach paste, which produces an attractive green colour – *lasagne verde* is a popular example; and with a proportion of tomato paste, which produces a deep coral-like colouring. *Pasta all'uovo*, which is made with the addition of eggs, is invariably produced in a range of flat shapes and those, too, are available in fresh and dried forms.

Coloured Pasta
As well as green pasta, coloured with spinach, and red pasta, made with tomato paste, there are other colours available: saffron pasta is an attractive yellow-orange colour, beetroot-coloured pasta is a deep pink, and pasta coloured with squid ink is a dramatic black. You can also buy or make pasta flecked with chopped basil and other herbs.

THE PASTA FAMILY

Pasta is generally divided into three main categories, long and folded pasta, noodles, and short pasta, the group that offers, perhaps, the greatest scope for inspired presentation and recipe variation.

   Since dried pasta has a shelf life of up to six months (see the panel on storage) and fresh pasta may be safely frozen for up to six months, it is a good idea to build up your own store cupboard of pasta selections to surprise and delight your family and friends.

Pasta Dictionary
The names of the various types and shapes of pasta have a romantic and evocative ring to them, conjuring up thoughts of warm, sunny climates and rich, herby sauces. But if you are not conversant with the similarities of

conversant with the similarities of tagliatelli and tagliarini, or the difference between cappelletti and conchiglie, you can find yourself longing for a translation. This glossary of some of the most popular pasta shapes should help you.

anelli and anellini rings small pasta used in soup

bozzoli deeply-ridged, cocoon-like shapes
bucatini long, medium-thick tubes

cappelletti wide-brimmed-hat shapes

cappelli d'angelo "angel's hair", thinner than cappellini

cappellini fine strands of ribbon pasta, usually sold curled into a nest shape

casareccia short curled lengths of pasta twisted at one end

cavatappi short, thick corkscrew shapes

conchiglie ridged shells

conchigliette little shells used in soup

cornetti ridged shells

cresti di gallo curved shapes, resembling cocks' combs

ditali, ditalini short tubes

eliche loose spiral shapes

elicoidali short, ridged tubes

farfalle butterflies
fedeli, fedelini fine tubes twisted into "skeins"

festonati short lengths, like garlands

fettuccine ribbon pasta, narrower than tagliatelle

fiochette, fiochelli small bow shapes
frezine broad, flat ribbons

fusilli spindles, or short spirals

fusilli bucati thin spirals, like springs

gemelli "twins", two pieces wrapped together

gramigna meaning "grass" or "weed"; the shapes look like sprouting seeds

lasagne flat, rectangular sheets

linguini long, flat ribbons

lumache smooth, snail-like shells

lumachine U-shaped flat noodles

macaroni, maccheroni long or short-cut tubes, may be ridged or elbow shapes

maltagliati triangular-shaped pieces, traditionally used in bean soups

noodles fine, medium or broad flat ribbons

orecchiette dished shapes; the word means "ear"

orzi tiny pasta, like grains of rice, used in soups

pappardelle widest ribbons, either straight or sawtooth-edged

pearlini tiny discs

penne short, thick tubes with diagonal-cut ends

pipe rigate ridged, curved pipe shapes

rigatoni thick, ridged tubes

ruoti wheels

semini seed shapes

Basic Pasta Dough cont.

3. Add the flour, semolina and salt and process until smooth. Sprinkle on a little more hot water if necessary to make the dough pliable. You can then transfer the dough to an electric mixer and knead for 2-3 minutes, using the dough hook.

4. Divide the dough into 2 equal pieces. Cover a working surface with a clean cloth or tea towel and dust it liberally with flour. Place one portion of the dough on the floured cloth and roll it out as thinly and evenly as possible, stretching the dough gently until the pattern of the weave shows through. Cover it with a cloth and roll out the second piece in a similar way.

5. Cut the dough into shapes of your choice. Use a ruler and a sharp knife blade to cut long, thin strips for noodles, or small confectionery cutters to cut rounds, stars or other decorative shapes.

6. Cover the dough shapes with a clean cloth and leave them in a cool place, not the refrigerator, for 30-45 minutes to become partly dry. Or place it in an airtight container for up to 24 hours.

7. Cook the fresh pasta in a large pan of boiling salted water, adding 1 tablespoon olive oil, for 3-4 minutes, until almost tender. Drain the pasta in a colander and serve with the sauce of your choice.

SPINACH & RICOTTA RAVIOLI

SERVES 4

1 recipe basic pasta dough (see above)
350 g/12 oz frozen spinach, thawed and chopped
175 g/6 oz/¾ cup Ricotta, or 90 g/3 oz each full-fat cream cheese and cottage cheese
4 tbsp grated Parmesan
salt and pepper
large pinch grated nutmeg

FOR THE SAUCE
25 g/1 oz/1 tbsp butter
150 ml/¼ pint/⅔ cup crème fraîche
grated nutmeg

1. Turn the chopped spinach into a colander and use a wooden spoon to press out as much of the liquid as possible.

2. Mix together the spinach and cheeses and season the mixture with salt, pepper and nutmeg. (For a smooth filling, you can mix the ingredients in a food processor.)

3. Divide the dough into two equal pieces and roll out each one as described on page 75. Cut one sheet into strips about 7.5cm/3in wide. Place small heaps of the filling at 7.5 cm/3 in intervals close to one side of each strip. Fold the strips over, press the edges to seal them and repeat with the remainder of the dough. Cut out the ravioli squares. A pastry wheel is useful for this, as it helps to seal the joins as it cuts.

continued opposite

semini seed shapes

spaghetti fine, medium or thick rods

spirale two rods twisted together into spirals

strozzapreti "priest strangler", double twisted strands

tagliarini flat, ribbon-like strips, thinner than tagliatelli

tagliatelli broad, flat ribbons

tortiglione thin, twisted tubes

vermicelli fine, slender strands usually sold folded into skeins

ziti tagliati short, thick tubes

Nutritional Value

Pasta has frequently had to answer to the charge that it is a fattening food to be avoided by anyone on a weight-reducing diet. The answer to that charge is that it may not be the pasta that piles on the calories, more likely some of the sauces we choose to serve with it.

This table will help you to sound out the dietary and nutritional credentials of dry pasta.

	per 100g
Average moisture content	11.10
Protein	13.20
Fat	2.80
Dietary fibre (approx.)	10.00
Starch (as monosaccharide)	65.70
Calories	327.00

Twisting and twirling

There is undoubtedly a knack to eating long spaghetti and other pasta strands. The timid may be tempted to cut the strands into short lengths and pick them up on a fork, but that is not the way the Italians do it.

You need a spoon or a soup spoon and a fork; no knife. Hold the fork in your right hand (if you are right-handed) and use it to pick up a bundle of spaghetti strands. Hold the spoon in your other hand, rest the prongs of the fork against the centre of the bowl and twirl the fork round, wrapping the spaghetti around it in a tight circle.

When there are no loose or dangling spaghetti strands, put the spoon down and convey the forkful of pasta deftly to your mouth. It is easy when you know how!

COOKING PASTA

The enjoyment of pasta depends on its being cooked to perfection; not too little, when it will be crisp and unyielding and taste of raw flour; not too much, when it will be too soft and the strands or shapes will probably stick together.

The Italians describe the perfect texture as *al dente*, meaning that the pasta is not quite tender, and still slightly resistant to the bite.

Cooking times vary according to the type and volume of the pasta, and you should always follow those recommended on the packet. In general, fresh pasta will be cooked in 3–5 minutes. Dried pasta becomes *al dente* in around 6 minutes for fine strands such as vermicelli; 7–12 minutes for quick-cooking macaroni, for spaghetti and noodles; and 10–15 minutes for cannelloni tubes and sheets of lasagne.

Whatever the pasta type, have ready a large pan of water at a steady, rolling boil. Add salt, and 1 tablespoon of olive oil, which will prevent the pieces from sticking together. Add the pasta gradually, a handful or a few strands at a time so that the water continues to boil. Hold the spaghetti and other long strands in one hand, lower it into the water and, as the pasta softens, twist the top so that the strands wind around the base of the pan.

Keep the water at a gentle, rolling boil. This action will help to prevent the pasta from sticking. Do not completely cover the pan, or the water will boil over. Leave it uncovered, or partly cover it with a tilted lid.

Drain the cooked pasta into a colander and, if it is not to be served at once, return it to the pan with a little butter or olive oil.

How much to allow

Appetites and occasions vary, and it is not possible to say exactly how much pasta to allow for each guest.
It is worth remembering that dried pasta more than doubles in volume during cooking, absorbing water or other liquid until it is rehydrated.

It is usual to allow 40-50 g/1-2 oz dried pasta per person for a first course or a salad, and 75-100 g/3-4 oz dried pasta for a main dish.

Crispy pasta fries

If you are serving pasta as an accompaniment to a main dish, and you have some left over, you might like to serve it as a crisply-fried snack.

Cut long strands such as spaghetti or macaroni into short lengths. Toss the pasta shapes with a fork to separate them.

Heat vegetable oil in a deep pan to moderately hot, 360deg.C/180deg.F, and drop in one piece of pasta. It should sizzle and turn brown within 30 seconds.

Fry the pasta in small batches, in a frying basket if you have one. If not, lift out the golden-brown pasta with a draining spoon, toss it on kitchen paper to dry and fry the remainder in a similar way.

Use the pasta as croûtons, as a garnish for soups; to scatter over green salad, or as a snack with drinks.

Storing and freezing pasta

Dried pasta will keep in good condition for up to six months. Keep it in the packet, and reseal it once you have opened it, or transfer the pasta to an airtight jar. You can buy tall glass spaghetti jars for long strands, and store other shapes decoratively in a row of glass-stopped jars.

Fresh pasta has a short storage life, only one or two days in the refrigerator, so buy it only when you want to serve it, and follow the advice on the packet.

Cooked pasta may be stored for up to three days in the refrigerator. If the pieces have stuck together, turn them in a colander and run warm water through them to separate them. Drain well, then toss the pasta in hot olive oil or melted butter before serving.

Freeze cooked pasta dishes in covered containers for up to 3 months. Thaw at room temperature before reheating.

Spinach & Ricotta Ravioli cont.

4. Cook the ravioli in a large pan of boiling water, to which you have added salt and 1 tbsp olive oil, for 3-4 minutes.

5. Heat together the butter and crème fraîche and season the sauce with salt, pepper and nutmeg.

6. Drain the pasta into a colander, turn it into a warmed serving dish and pour over the sauce. Toss the ravioli to coat it thoroughly.

TOMATO SAUCE

2 tbsp olive oil
1 small onion, chopped
1 garlic clove, chopped
1 x 424 g/15 oz can chopped tomatoes
2 tbsp chopped parsley
1 tsp dried oregano
2 bay leaves
2 tbsp tomato purée (paste)
1 tsp sugar

1. To make the tomato sauce, heat the oil in a pan over a medium heat and fry the onion until it is translucent. Add the garlic and fry for 1 further minute.

2. Stir in the chopped tomatoes, parsley, oregano, bay leaves, tomato purée (paste) and sugar and bring the sauce to the boil.

3.Simmer, uncovered, until the sauce has reduced by half, about15-20 minutes. Taste the sauce and adjust the seasoning if necessary. Discard the bay leaves.

BECHAMEL SAUCE

300 ml/¹/₂ pint/ 1¹/₄ cups milk
2 bay leaves
3 cloves
1 small onion
60 g/ 2 oz/ ¹/₄ cup butter, plus
*   extra for greasing*
45 g/ 1¹/₂ oz/ 6 tbsp flour
300 ml/¹/₂ pint/ 1¹/₄ cups single
*   cream*
large pinch of grated nutmeg
salt and pepper

1. Pour the milk into a small pan and add bay leaves. Press the cloves into the onion, add to the pan and bring the milk to the boil. Remove from the heat and set it aside to cool.

2. Strain the milk into a jug and rinse the pan. Melt the butter in the pan and stir in the flour. Stir for 1 minute, then gradually pour on the milk, stirring constantly. Cook the sauce for 3 minutes, then pour on the cream and bring it to the boil. Remove from the heat and season with nutmeg, salt and pepper.

CHEESE SAUCE

30 g/ 1 oz/ 2 tbsp butter
1 tbsp flour
250 ml/ 8 fl oz/ 1 cup milk
2 tbsp single cream
pinch of grated nutmeg
45 g/ 1¹/₂ oz Cheddar cheese,
*   grated*
1 tbsp grated Parmesan cheese

1. Melt the butter in a pan, stir in the flour and cook for 1 minute.
continued opposite

PASTA MACHINES

Pasta machines that will stretch and roll the dough are now widely available. You will need plenty of space for the rolled-out dough, as well as somewhere to hang the dough to dry, once it has been cut.

The correct technique is to feed the pasta through the rollers one notch at a time. This is time-consuming but important, as the pasta needs to be thinned gradually so that it keeps its elasticity.

To roll the pasta from the recipe on page 74, first divide the dough into 2 pieces. If the pasta strip becomes too long and unwieldy as it stretches, cut it again. Roll until all the pieces have gone through the machine at each setting, from the highest down to the thinnest. Lay out the pasta on tea towels to dry.

Leave the pasta to dry until it feels leathery before you attempt to cut it, though it must not be so dry that it is brittle. The machine will cut pasta into strips for ribbon pasta; other shapes will have to be cut by hand. To use pasta strips immediately, place a tea towel over the back of a chair and hang the strips there to dry. Traditionally, a broom handle was stretched across the room, and the pasta hung over it.

PASTA SAUCES

Getting to know the individual pasta shapes is one of the delights of this form of cookery, and creative cooks will enjoy partnering their favourite sauces with first one and then another type of pasta. Although there are classic combinations such as Spaghetti Bolognese, when the pasta is tossed with the rich meat and tomato sauce of southern Italy, and Spaghetti Carbonara, when the eggs in the sauce are cooked on contact with the piping hot pasta, there are no hard and fast rules, just guidelines.

These guidelines are largely a matter of practicality. Long slender strands of pasta combine well with meat, fish and vegetable sauces, without absorbing the liquid element or concealing the shape and texture of the principal ingredient. Twisted, curved and hollow pasta shapes are ideal to serve with runny sauces, which get deliciously trapped in, say, the cavities of large pasta shells, and small shapes and fine strands are especially good for adding body and texture to clear meat, fish and vegetable soups.

Appearance is a factor in creating partnerships of pasta and sauce. Shells are an obvious example, to evoke the appropriate mental image when combined with fish and seafoods. Taste comes into the decision-making process too. It may seem improbable, but it is a fact that spaghetti tossed with a green vegetable sauce does taste different from, say, pasta wagon wheels served with the identical sauce. And a calamares stew would lose much of its robust character if it were made with tiny pasta stars instead of macaroni.

Cheeses with Pasta
Some cheeses have a natural affinity with pasta dishes and appear frequently in recipes. It is always worth having a supply in store, handy for use at short notice. If you have difficulty in buying

Parmesan in a whole piece, try a good Italian food store or delicatessen.

Ricotta A milky white, soft and crumbly Italian cheese which resembles cottage cheese. It is low in fat, being traditionally made from whey, but some varieties produced now have a proportion of whole milk added. If you cannot obtain Ricotta, use another low-fat soft cheese, or cottage cheese. To obtain a smooth-textured sauce or filling press cottage cheese through a sieve.

Parmesan A mature and exceptionally hard cheese produced in Italy. Parmesan, properly known as Parmigiano-reggiano, plays such an important part in the overall flavour of pasta dishes that it is worth exploiting its potential to the full. It may be useful to have a small carton of ready-grated Parmesan in the refrigerator, but you will find that it quickly loses its characteristic pungency and "bite". For that reason, it is better to buy small quantities of the cheese in one piece (it is usually very expensive) and grate it yourself as needed. Tightly wrapped in cling film and foil, it will keep in the refrigerator for several months. Grate it just before serving, for maximum flavour. To grate a large quantity by hand is time-consuming, as the cheese is so hard: you may find it easier to use a food processor.

Pecorino A hard sheep's milk cheese which resembles Parmesan and is often used for grating over dishes. It has a sharp flavour and is only used in small quantities. Best bought in the piece and stored, tightly wrapped in cling film and foil, in the refrigerator.

Mozzarella Another highly popular cheese, often found in pasta dishes. It is a soft, fresh cheese, with a piquant flavour, traditionally made from water buffalo's milk, and is usually sold surrounded by whey to keep it moist. Buffalo milk is now scarce, and so nowadays this cheese is often made with cow's milk. It can be used fresh, most popularly in tomato salads, and is also often added to provide a tangy, chewy layer to baked dishes.

OLIVE OIL

Olive oil, which is at the heart of so many pasta dishes, has a personality all of its own, and each variety has its own characteristic flavour. The main oil-producing countries are Italy, Greece and Spain. It is important to be able to recognize the different grades of oil.

Extra-virgin olive oil This is the finest grade, made from the first, cold pressing of hand gathered olives. Always use extra-virgin oil for salad dressings.

Virgin olive oil This oil has a fine aroma and colour, and is also made by cold pressing. It may have a slightly higher acidity level than extra-virgin oil.

Refined or "pure" olive oil This is made by treating the paste residue from the pressings with heat or solvents to remove the residual oil.

Olive oil is a blend of refined and virgin olive oil.

Cheese Sauce cont.

2. Gradually pour on the milk, stirring all the time. Stir in the cream and season the sauce with nutmeg, salt and pepper.

3. Simmer the sauce for 5 minutes to reduce, then remove it from the heat and stir in the cheeses. Stir until the cheese has melted and blended into the sauce.

LAMB SAUCE

2 tbsp olive oil
1 large onion, sliced
2 celery stalks, thinly sliced
500 g/1 lb lean lamb, minced
3 tbsp tomato purée (paste)
150 g/5 oz bottled sun-dried
    tomatoes, drained and chopped
1 tsp dried oregano
1 tbsp red wine vinegar
150 ml/^{1}/$_4$ pint/^{2}/$_3$ cup chicken
    stock
salt and pepper

1. Heat the oil in the frying pan over a medium heat and fry the onion and celery until the onion is translucent. Add the lamb, stirring frequently, and fry until it changes colour.

2. Stir in the tomato purée (paste), sun-dried tomatoes, oregano, wine vinegar and stock and season with salt and pepper.

3. Bring the sauce to the boil and cook, uncovered, for about 20 minutes until the meat has absorbed the stock. Taste the sauce and adjust the seasoning if necessary.

INDEX